A Little Bit of
GOLFING
WIT

Tom Hay

summersdale

A LITTLE BIT OF GOLFING WIT

This updated edition copyright © Summersdale Publishers Ltd, 2018
First published in 2010

With research by Aubrey Malone

Illustrations by Ian Baker
Golf ball icons © Marie Nimrichterova/Shutterstock.com

Summersdale Publishers Ltd
46 West Street
Chichester
West Sussex
PO19 1RP
UK

www.summersdale.com

Printed and bound in Malta

ISBN: 978-1-78685-250-2

Substantial discounts on bulk quantities of Summersdale books are available to corporations, professional associations and other organisations. For details contact general enquiries: telephone: +44 (0) 1243 771107 or email: enquiries@summersdale.com.

CONTENTS

EDITOR'S NOTE

As Peter Dobereiner once said, 'Everyone gets wounded in a game of golf. The trick is not to bleed.' There can be no denying that, despite all its purported sophistication and gentlemanly conduct, a bad round of golf can be a killer – and while they may not help you get that all-important hole-in-one, this collection of quips and quotes for the golf-obsessed will certainly give you something to laugh about after one too many bogeys.

So when it's your turn to buy everyone drinks at the nineteenth, put your best ball forward and dig deep into this little compendium of golfing treasures to find the perfect one-liner for any occasion.

WHAT IS GOLF?

Golf is a game in which players lie
about their scores to people who
used to be their friends.

ANONYMOUS

Golf was never meant to be
an exact science. Einstein
was lousy at it.

BOB TOSKI

GOLF IS SOMEWHERE BETWEEN MAKING LOVE AND WRITING A POEM.

John Updike

The loneliest of all games,
not excluding postal chess.

PETER DOBEREINER

Golf's not that hard.
The ball doesn't move.

TED WILLIAMS

Golf is not a funeral, though both
can be very sad affairs.

BERNARD DARWIN

Golf is not a sport. Golf is men
in ugly pants, walking.

ROSIE O'DONNELL

THE GAME WAS INVENTED FOR SIMPLETONS.

Spike Milligan

HIT AND MRS

Footballers' wives fall out of
taxis blathered. The worst
a golf wife does is wear an
uncoordinated dress.

ANONYMOUS

Many men are more faithful
to their golf partners than to
their wives and have stuck
with them longer.

JOHN UPDIKE

Husband: I got a new set
of clubs for my wife.
Friend: That sounds like
a fair swap.

BILL WANNAN

Golf is wrecking my head.
Yesterday I kissed my seven-iron
goodbye and putted my wife.

DON RICKLES

ONE OF JOB'S CHIEF TRIALS WAS THAT HIS WIFE INSISTED ON PLAYING GOLF WITH HIM.

P. G. Wodehouse

I plan to be a golf widow next week. I've just bought the gun.

JOAN RIVERS

Our relationship lasted longer than either of his two marriages.

NICK FALDO'S COACH DAVID LEADBETTER, WHO WAS SACKED BY FALDO AFTER 13 YEARS

You can take a man's wife.
You can even take his wallet.
But never on any account
take his putter.

ARCHIE COMPSTON

My putter worked so well...
I'm going to sleep with it tonight.
My husband will have to
go next door.

JOANNE CARNER

THE CRUEL
GAME

I thought about taking up golf...
and then I thought again.

GROUCHO MARX

Give me a man with big hands,
big feet and no brains... I will
make a golfer out of him.

WALTER HAGEN

Golf is the cruellest of sports…
It plays with men. And runs off
with the butcher.

JIM MURRAY

I've never been depressed enough
to take up the game.

WILL ROGERS

EVERYONE GETS WOUNDED IN A GAME OF GOLF. THE TRICK IS NOT TO BLEED.

Peter Dobereiner

GOLF HAS GIVEN ME AN UNDERSTANDING OF THE FUTILITY OF LIFE.

Aubrey Eban

You learn a lot about yourself by
playing golf. Unfortunately, most
of it is unprintable.

BURT LANCASTER

I've been playing golf for 20 years
now and have just made
a discovery. I hate it.

REX BEACH

THE NINETEENTH HOLE

What scoundrel took the cork
out of my lunch?

W. C. FIELDS DURING A 'SNACK' BREAK
AT THE LAKESIDE CLUB IN LA

My favourite hole was always
the watering hole.

RONAN RAFFERTY

First time I played the Masters...
I drank a bottle of rum... I shot
the happiest 83 of my life.

CHI-CHI RODRÍGUEZ

Scotland is the birthplace of golf...
which may explain why it is also
the birthplace of whisky.

HENRY BEARD

The nineteenth hole is the only
one where players can have as
many shots as they like.

LOUIS SAFIAN

If you drink, don't drive.
Don't even putt.

DEAN MARTIN

THE BARTENDER IN THE CLUBHOUSE HEARS SO MANY STORIES ABOUT MISSED OPPORTUNITIES AND FAILED LIVES, HE COULD CHARGE ANALYSIS FEES.

Robert Powell

GOLF
TIPS

The secret of missing a tree is to aim straight for it.

MICHAEL GREEN

Golf should never be played on any day with a 'y' in it.

LES DAWSON

I JUST LOOSEN MY GIRDLE AND LET IT FLY.

Babe Didrikson Zaharias on how she hits the ball so far

One may do you good, but if you swallow the whole bottle you'll be lucky to survive.

HARVEY PENICK ON HOW GOLF TIPS ARE LIKE ASPIRIN

Never give up a hole. Quitting between tee and green is more habit-forming than drinking highballs before breakfast.

SAM SNEAD

Never try to keep more than 300 separate thoughts in your mind during your swing.

HENRY BEARD

Hit it a bloody sight harder!

TED RAY AFTER A NOVICE ASKED HIM HOW HE MIGHT GET THE BALL TO TRAVEL FURTHER

PLAY THE SHOT AT HAND – NOT THE LAST ONE, NOT THE NEXT ONE, BUT THE ONE AT YOUR FEET, IN THE POISON IVY, WHERE YOU PUT IT.

John Updike

PRACTICE MAKES PERFECT

They call me a natural player.
So why do I have to practise till
my hands bleed?

SEVE BALLESTEROS

When Julius Boros putts, you
can't tell by looking whether he's...
practising or it's fifty grand
if he sinks it.

LEE TREVINO

I hate practice; my idea of warming up is a double egg, sausage, bacon and fried bread.

MICHAEL PARKINSON

Golf teaches us that although practice doesn't always make perfect, no practice always makes us imperfect.

THOM HARTMAN

I have taught golf at a driving-range... and have seen many people actually practising mistakes.

MEL FLANAGAN

I don't practise much these days. At my age, you need to keep all your energy for your actual shots.

SAM SNEAD AT 78

I'VE BEEN PRACTISING MY SWING IN FRONT OF THE MIRROR FOR A FEW MONTHS AND IT'S WORKING A TREAT.

John Denver

LET'S PUTT IT LIKE THIS

Whoever said putting was
a pleasure obviously
never played golf.

MICHAEL GREEN

★ ★ ★ ★ ★ ★ ★

Do that again and you'll
wear my putter.

BOB SHEARER TO A PHOTOGRAPHER WHO
DISTRACTED HIM WHILE PLAYING A SHOT IN 1975

Putt in haste and
repent at leisure.

GERALD BATCHELOR

I think I know the answer to your
putting problems. You need to hit
the ball closer to the hole.

**VALERIE HOGAN TO HER LEGENDARY
HUSBAND BEN**

I WAS PUTTING LIKE A LOBOTOMISED BABOON.

Tony Johnstone

I STILL HAVE THE PUTTER WITH WHICH I MISSED THAT TWO-AND-A-HALF-FOOT PUTT TO WIN THE OPEN. IT'S IN TWO PIECES.

Doug Sanders

The only time Clayton
Heafner could putt was when
he got mad enough to hate
the ball into the hole.

CARY MIDDLECOFF

There are three things
a man must do alone:
testify, die, and putt.

BENNETT CERF

To 'put' is to place
something somewhere.
To 'putt' is to fail to do so.

GARY KOCH

Tommy Bolt's putters spent more
time in the air than Lindberg.

JIMMY DEMARET

WHEN YOU'RE PUTTING BADLY YOU CAN HEAR A MAN JINGLE TWO COINS IN HIS POCKET 100 YARDS AWAY.

Tony Jacklin

THE LESS SAID ABOUT THE PUTTER THE BETTER. HERE IS AN INSTRUMENT OF TORTURE, DESIGNED BY TANTALUS AND FORGED IN THE DEVIL'S OWN SMITHY.

Tony Lema

ER, COME AGAIN?

I would like to thank the press from the heart of my bottom.

NICK FALDO

★ ★ ★ ★ ★ ★ ★

Ninety-five per cent of putts which finish short don't go in.

ROBERT GREEN

Seve Ballesteros is relaxed in
an intense sort of way.

COLIN MONTGOMERIE

I must play less in order to
prolong my career.

SEVE BALLESTEROS

MY 15 MINUTES OF FAME RAN TO ALMOST A DECADE.

Laura Baugh

NICK FALDO THIS AFTERNOON IS ALL IN BLUE, WITH A WHITE SHIRT.

Tony Adamson

So, Woosie, you're from Wales.
What part of Scotland is that?

**AMERICAN JOURNALIST TO IAN WOOSNAM
DURING A 1987 PRESS CONFERENCE**

Piñero has missed the putt.
I wonder what he's
thinking in Spanish.

RENTON LAIDLAW

I'M LEARNING NOT TO GET TOO EXCITED AFTER ONE GOOD ROUND AND TO KEEP MY HEAD ON THE GROUND.

Colin Montgomerie

MAGNIFICENT OBSESSION

What is love compared to holing
out before your opponent?

P. G. WODEHOUSE

Golfers are a level-headed lot.
They only talk about golf three
times a day: before they play,
while they're playing, and
after they've played.

KATHARINE WHITEHORN

Golf is my profession.
Show business is just to
pay the green fees.

BOB HOPE

Real golfers go to work to relax.

GEORGE DILLON

You know you're a bit weird when
you ask for *Golf Digest* bedtime
stories at three.

JOHN ELLIS

Golf is not a relaxation.
Golf is a religion.

BOB REID

CLOTHES
LINES

I'd give up golf if I didn't have
so many sweaters.

BOB HOPE

I had to change into brown
trousers after playing my first
hole at the Masters.

TREVOR HOMER

THE GOLFING GIRL OF TODAY SHOULD INDEED BE GRATEFUL THAT SHE NEED NOT PLAY IN A SAILOR HAT.

Mabel Stringer

I hope you're wearing
that for a bet.

COLIN MONTGOMERIE TO PAYNE STEWART

I was asked to leave my last one
because my socks weren't colour
coordinated with my umbrella.

**MILDRED SASSOON ON THE
FUSSINESS OF GOLF CLUBS**

My God, I've got socks
older than you.

LEE TREVINO TO A 27-YEAR-OLD OPPONENT

I have known girls to become
golfers as an excuse to
wear pink jumpers.

P. G. WODEHOUSE

I'LL TAKE A TWO-SHOT PENALTY, BUT I'LL BE DAMNED IF I'M GOING TO PLAY THE BALL WHERE IT LIES.

Elaine Johnson after her tee–shot
rebounded off a tree and ended
up in her bra

WEIGHT
WATCHERS

If it wasn't for golf, I'd probably be the fat lady in the circus now.

KATHY WHITWORTH

Most of the guys on the tour are built like truck drivers but have the touch of hairdressers.

CLAYTON HEAFNER

It takes a lot of guts to play
golf... look at Billy Casper...
he has a lot of guts.

GARY PLAYER

I've lost 40 pounds since
Christmas – 150 if you
include the wife.

DAVID FEHERTY

Some guys try to shoot their age.
Craig Stadler tries to shoot
his weight.

JIM MURRAY

Golf and cricket are the only two
games where you can actually
put on weight while playing them.

TOMMY DOCHERTY

CONUNDRUMS

Why is it called a three-wood
when it's made out of metal?

ERNIE WITHAM

One day you play really well and
the next really crap – and you
don't know why.

PATRICK RAYNER

If the universe is finite... how come golfers never find all the balls they lose?

HAL ROACH

Is it any accident that 'God' comes just before 'golf' in the dictionary?

DAVE ALLEN

IF GOLF IS A RICH MAN'S GAME, HOW COME THERE ARE SO MANY POOR PLAYERS?

Mitch Murray

HERE'S
TO THE
LOSERS

Few things draw two men together more than a mutual inability to play golf.

P. G. WODEHOUSE

I have often been gratefully aware of the heroic efforts of my opponents not to laugh at me.

BERNARD DARWIN

The only thing I ever learned from losing was that I don't like it.

TOM WATSON

There are 2,000 different ways you can hit the ball wrong. So far I think I've reached about 1,800.

DINAH SHORE

Defeat is worse than death,
because you have to live
with defeat.

NICK FALDO

Golf.

JACKIE GLEASON AFTER BEING ASKED
WHAT HIS HANDICAP WAS

Show me a good loser and I'll
show you a loser.

GARY PLAYER

I play golf like Cinderella. I never
make it to the ball.

DON RICKLES

I WOULDN'T KNOW A NINE-IRON FROM A STEAM IRON.

Lise Hand

The worse you play, the
better you remember the
occasional good shot.

NUBAR GULBENKIAN

My most notable trait is snatching
defeat out of the jaws of victory.

DOUG SANDERS

I played so badly I got a 'get well'
card from the Inland Revenue.

JOHNNY MILLER

I achieved a lot by climbing over
113 golfers. The only problem was
that there were 114 ahead of me.

JOANNE CARNER

WE COULDN'T HIT A COW'S ARSE WITH A BANJO.

Mark James on the Ryder Cup team in 1977

CADDYSHACK

The first thing to understand about caddying is that it's not brain surgery. It's much more complicated than that.

LAWRENCE DONEGAN

I asked Marilyn Monroe if she'd come golfing... 'I can't,' she said, 'I don't even know how to hold the caddy.'

DEAN MARTIN

Real golfers... never strike a caddy with the driver. The sand wedge is infinitely more effective.

HUXTABLE PIPPEY

Divorces between caddies and players are often executed on the spot, and there isn't any alimony.

JOHN O'REILLY

Golfer to caddy after messing
up a shot: Golf is a funny
old game, innit?
Caddy: The way you play it,
it certainly is, sir.

GREG DOHERTY

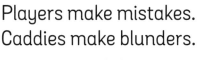

Players make mistakes.
Caddies make blunders.

JERRY OSBORN

GOLFER: DO YOU THINK I CAN GET THERE WITH A FIVE-IRON? CADDY: EVENTUALLY.

Anonymous

SANDBAGGERS

Lawrence of Arabia, Tarbuck of
Las Brisas… when you speak of
sand, we have been there.

JIMMY TARBUCK

A sand trap is a deep depression
of sand, filled with golfers in
deep depressions.

HENRY BEARD

There's no rule against your standing over him and counting his strokes aloud with increasing gusto.

HORACE G. HUTCHINSON ON WHEN YOUR OPPONENT IS STUCK IN A BUNKER

At my age it's tough trying to get out of the bunkers. I mean after I've hit the ball.

GEORGE BURNS

I never kick my ball in the rough
or improve my lie in a sand trap.
For that I have a caddy.

BOB HOPE

I call golf 'Connect the
Sand Traps'.

JACK BENNY

THE EGOS
HAVE
LANDED

There are days when you feel you
can't miss even when you try to.

JACK NICKLAUS

Any time I get ideas above
my station my wife says,
'Put the garbage out.'

SANDY LYLE

If I didn't sign autographs while
I was walking, I'd never make
my tee-off time.

COLIN MONTGOMERIE

I never miss-hit a shot. Every
drive was perfect, and every iron.
I was in awe of myself.

GREG NORMAN AFTER WINNING
THE BRITISH OPEN

If I can hit it I can hole it.

ARNOLD PALMER

Arnold Palmer doesn't so much walk onto the first tee as climb into it... as though it were a prize ring.

CHARLES PRICE

IT WAS SO GOOD I COULD NEARLY FEEL THE BABY APPLAUDING.

A seven–months–pregnant Donna White after a good putt

My driving is so good these days
I have to dial the operator long
distance after I hit it.

LEE TREVINO

I always ask my caddy to tell me
two things: the yardage, and that
I'm the best in the world.

JACK NICKLAUS

All of us believe that our good
shots are the norm, and our bad
ones aberrations.

ALEC MORRISON

One minute it's fear and loathing,
but hit a couple of good shots and
you feel like God.

JACK NICHOLSON

LET'S GET PHYSICAL

A true pro always prefers his golf course to his intercourse.

CONAN O'BRIEN

My wife gave me ten oysters last night to rouse my passion, but only nine of them worked.

LEE TREVINO

I WISH IT HAD BITTEN ME A LITTLE LOWER DOWN.

David Feherty, whose arm swelled up to twice its normal size after being bitten by a snake at Wentworth

Would you say a golfer is a man
who putts it about?

BEN ELTON

Golf groupies must be the most
passive of any competitive game.
Even chess fans display
greater vivacity.

ROBERT O'BYRNE

THE
ICONS

Nick Faldo's idea of excitement
is having his After Eight
mints at 7.30.

GRAHAM ELLIOT

Tiger Woods has such a lazy style;
last week I caught him nodding
off on his backswing.

ANONYMOUS

Arnold Palmer would go for
the flag from the middle of
an alligator's back.

LEE TREVINO

John Daly could draw a crowd
in Saskatchewan.

ROCCO MEDIATE

SEVE BALLESTEROS HITS THE BALL FARTHER THAN I GO ON MY HOLIDAYS.

Lee Trevino

Big Four – Palmer, Nicklaus, Player and Trevino. I just want to be the fifth wheel in case somebody gets a flat.

CHI-CHI RODRÍGUEZ

Maybe I should dye my hair peroxide blonde and call myself The Great White Tadpole.

IAN WOOSNAM ON HOW HE MIGHT CREATE A REMARKABLE IMAGE FOR HIMSELF

In the real world a bad week is
waking up and finding you're a
steelworker in Scunthorpe.

NICK FALDO

Jack Nicklaus is a legend
in his spare time.

TOM WATSON

BYE, BYE, BIRDIE

I gave up golf for painting because
it takes me less strokes.

DWIGHT D. EISENHOWER

I know exactly when I want to
retire now, but when I reach
that time I may not.

JACK NICKLAUS

MEN CHASE GOLF BALLS WHEN THEY'RE TOO OLD TO CHASE ANYTHING ELSE.

Groucho Marx

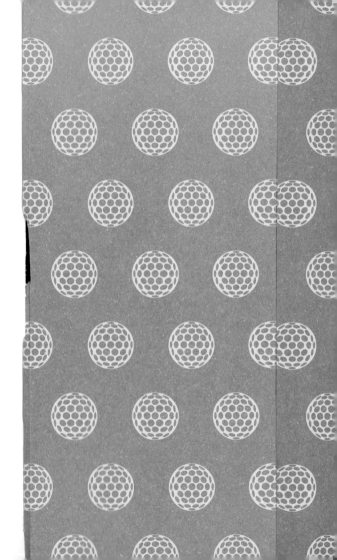

If you're interested in finding out more about our books, find us on Facebook at **Summersdale Publishers** and follow us on Twitter at **@Summersdale**.

www.summersdale.com

If you're interested in finding out more about our books, find us on Facebook at **Summersdale Publishers** and follow us on Twitter at **@Summersdale**.

www.summersdale.com